EXPERIENCING
GOD'S ATTRIBUTES

Warren and Ruth Myers

NAVPRESS®

Bringing Truth to Life

OUR GUARANTEE TO YOU

We believe so strongly in the message of our books that we are making this quality guarantee to you. If for any reason you are disappointed with the content of this book, return the title page to us with your name and address and we will refund to you the list price of the book. To help us serve you better, please briefly describe why you were disappointed. Mail your refund request to: NavPress, P.O. Box 35002, Colorado Springs, CO 80935.

NavPress
P.O. Box 35001
Colorado Springs, Colorado 80935

The Navigators is an international Christian organization. Our mission is to reach, disciple, and equip people to know Christ and to make Him known through successive generations. We envision multitudes of diverse people in the United States and every other nation who have a passionate love for Christ, live a lifestyle of sharing Christ's love, and multiply spiritual laborers among those without Christ.

NavPress is the publishing ministry of The Navigators. NavPress publications help believers learn biblical truth and apply what they learn to their lives and ministries. Our mission is to stimulate spiritual formation among our readers.

ISBN 1-57683-419-0

Cover design by Ray Moore
Cover photo by Byron Aughenbaugh
Creative Team: Paul Santhouse, Keith Wall, Darla Hightower, Pat Miller

Some of the anecdotal illustrations in this book are true to life and are included with the permission of the persons involved. All other illustrations are composites of real situations, and any resemblance to people living or dead is coincidental.

Unless otherwise identified, all Scripture quotations in this publication are taken from the *New American Standard Bible* (NASB), © The Lockman Foundation 1960, 1962, 1963, 1968, 1971, 1972, 1973, 1975, 1977. Other versions include: *The New Testament in Modern English* (PH), J. B. Phillips Translator, © J. B. Phillips 1958, 1960, 1965, used by permission of Macmillan Publishing Company; *The Living Bible* (TLB), Copyright © 1971, used by permission of Tyndale House Publishers, Inc., Wheaton, IL 60189, all rights reserved; the *Amplified New Testament* (AMP), © The Lockman Foundation 1954, 1958; the *Modern Language Bible: The Berkeley Version in Modern English* (MLB), copyright © 1945, 1959, 1969 by Zondervan Publishing House, used by permission; and the *King James Version* (KJV).

Printed in Canada

1 2 3 4 5 6 7 8 9 10 / 07 06 05 04 03

CONTENTS

AS YOU
BEGIN

HOW ACCURATE IS MY concept of God? How well do I really know Him? Are my feelings about Him based on what He is truly like? An honest evaluation will reveal my need to know God better, and a true knowledge of God is the greatest factor in living realistically in this world.

For God is Ultimate Reality. He should be the solid foundation on which we rest, the goal toward which we press, and the never-failing power by which we live. As we learn to view everything in light of who He is, we form reliable viewpoints regarding ourselves, others, and the nature of life itself. To know God better is our deepest need.

God longs to reveal Himself to us and He does so in many ways. The heavens declare His glory, and we can sense His greatness in a dazzling sunset. People who know Him radiate His beauty as they live in vital touch with Him, and we can feel His warmth as we mingle with those who channel His love to us.

But to know Him deeply and accurately, we must come with seeking hearts to the Bible. Here in the Scriptures He unveils Himself most clearly. Here He has revealed to us His thoughts, which are higher than ours as the heavens are higher than the earth (see Isaiah 55:8-9) He has clothed these unsearchable thoughts in human words, available for us to read and understand, so that we can know the limitless God in a true, though limited, way.

In the Scriptures God has given us a portrait of Himself. As we pray for a spirit of wisdom and revelation in the knowledge of Him and search for Him as for hidden treasure, we will see Him not only in the passages that describe His attributes, but on every page of our Bibles. The biblical narratives show Him involved with men and women, meeting human needs; the commands reveal what He approves; the promises portray what He wants to do for us. In the Gospels we see the Father's character as we look at Jesus. ④ And prophecies show God's long-range purposes and His ultimate triumph.

Knowing God, however, involves more than accumulating facts about Him. To know God is to understand Him and experience Him daily in worship, dependence, and obedience. It is finding Him adequate for every need. "The people that do know their God shall be strong, and do exploits" (Daniel 11:32, KJV).

Truly knowing God provides an unshakable foundation *to take advantage of* for living and for serving Him effectively. When we base our lives on our feelings and abilities, on others' evaluations of us, or on Satan's lies, we live parched, uncertain lives full of frustration and discouragement. Or we project a self-mastery that glorifies us rather than God, until eventually reality breaks through and forces us to face our human limitations and emptiness. In contrast, as we learn to live on the solid facts of who God is, our lives become stable, joyful, and victorious. God describes this contrast vividly:

> Cursed is the man who trusts in man and makes flesh his arm, whose heart
> departs from the LORD. He is like a juniper tree in a desert and shall not be
> aware when good comes; he shall inhabit the parched places in the wilder-
> ness, an uninhabited salt land. *Ps 40:3, Pr 16:20*
>
> ✓¹ Blessed is the man who (trusts) in the LORD, and whose confidence is
> the LORD. He is like a tree planted by water, that sends out its roots by the
> stream, and it does not fear when heat comes, for its leaves remain green;
> in the year of drought it is not anxious, for it does not fail to yield fruit.
>
> —JEREMIAH 17:5-8, MLB

If we want these benefits of consistent trust in the Lord, a casual investigation of the Bible will not do. Rather, we must seek wholeheartedly a deeper knowledge of Him in His Word. By persistent choice we must make Him the major pursuit of our lives, following the examples of men like Moses, David, and Paul, who pursued Him above all else (see Exodus 33:13,18; Psalm 27:4; Philippians 3:10).

As we seek God, we must also *depend* on Him today on the basis of what we already know about Him. We don't have to wait until we know Him better to rely on Him. Yet as we do get to know Him better, our dependence will become deeper and more constant.

We can always be knowing God more.

As we contemplate God in His Word, the blend of qualities in His character amazes us: unlimited strength and utmost tenderness, majestic glory and infinite mercy, uncompromising justice and unqualified forgiveness. His holy love for us **✱ powerful Truth.** stands undiminished in spite of His total knowledge of us as imperfect persons.

This thirteen-part Bible-study workbook will help you examine some of God's amazing attributes and then apply their lessons to your own life. As you take time to consider the marvelous ways these qualities come together in His character, you will find yourself trusting Him more consistently, worshiping Him more completely, and sharing Him with others more freely.

As you study, avoid two extremes: the strictly intellectual approach that merely accumulates correct mental notions about God and the simply experiential approach that is preoccupied with elated religious experiences. Knowing God properly means **√|** experiencing Him with your mind *and* your will *and* your emotions. This is what Paul wrote to the Colossians: "How I long for you to grow more certain in your knowledge and more sure in your grasp of God Himself. May your spiritual experience become richer as you see more and more fully God's great secret, Christ Himself! For it is in Him, and in Him alone, that men will find all the treasures of wisdom and knowledge" (Colossians 2:2-3, PH). Don't settle for less.

> O God, You are my God; I shall seek You earnestly;
> My soul thirsts for You, my flesh yearns for You,
> In a dry and weary land where there is no water.
> Thus I have seen You in the sanctuary,
> To see Your power and Your glory.
> Because Your lovingkindness is better than life,
> My lips will praise You.
>
> —PSALM 63:1-3

> [For my determined purpose is] that I may know Him [that I may progressively become more deeply and intimately acquainted with Him, perceiving and recognizing and understanding the wonders of His Person more strongly and more clearly.]
>
> —PHILIPPIANS 3:10, AMP

O God, I have tasted Thy goodness, and it has both satisfied me and made me thirsty for more. I am painfully conscious of my need of further grace. I am ashamed of my lack of desire. O God, the Triune God, I want to want Thee; I long to be filled with longing; I thirst to be made more thirsty still. Show me Thy glory, I pray Thee, that so I may know Thee indeed. Begin in mercy a new work of love within me. Say to my soul, "Rise up, my love, my fair one, and come away." Then give me grace to rise and follow Thee up from this misty lowland where I have wandered so long. In Jesus' name, Amen.

—A. W. Tozer[1]

NOTE: This study does not attempt to explore the doctrine of God exhaustively. Its purpose is to focus on particular attributes of God for your study and meditation, with a view to personal spiritual enrichment. Other facets of truth about God will appear in other studies in the *Experiencing God Series*.

---

1. A. W. Tozer, *The Pursuit of God* (Harrisburg, Penn.: Christian Publications, Inc., 1948), p. 20.

HOW TO DO THE
EXPERIENCING GOD STUDY

T HIS BIBLE STUDY AND meditation series has been designed to open for you new and exciting avenues of biblical understanding and to help you apply the truths you discover. Each topic is divided into two studies. The first section, *Experiencing God Study,* will begin to give you a rich grasp of an attribute of God. The optional *Additional Experiencing God Study* will enable you to study and understand the attribute in a deeper way.

In order to discover and apply these truths about the person of God, you will have to spend time meditating and praying over the Scripture passages. Approach the study expectantly, relying on the Holy Spirit to guide you in your desire to know God better. The most profitable way of doing this study is to do it yourself first, then meet with a group that has also done it and discuss your discoveries and applications with one another.

AIDS TO YOUR STUDY

Use a basic Bible version, such as the *King James Version,* the *New American Standard Bible,* the *New International Version,* or the *Revised Standard Version* as your main Bible. You can then enrich your study by also referring to one or more of the other versions and paraphrases presently available, such as *The Message* by Eugene Peterson, *The New Testament in Modern English* by J. B. Phillips, the *Modern Language Bible* (Berkeley), the *New English Bible,* and *The New Living Translation.*

(For additional materials that can help you in personal meditation and Bible study, and in group discussion, see *For Further Reading,* page 101.)

Adjust the time you spend in study to your personal time requirements and needs. Begin with the *Experiencing God Study* section and then go on to the *Additional Experiencing God Study* if you desire to pursue the topic further.

You may want to keep a notebook with space to record longer answers, prayer requests, illustrations, and personal observations on the study material.

PARTS OF YOUR STUDY

Each study section is divided into five parts. Before you begin your first study, reread the *As You Begin* section of this book, marking the truths that stand out to you and reviewing them each time you do a study.

Following are the instructions for each part of the study.

1. VERSES TO CONSIDER

The Bible verses listed in this part are the ones you will use for the attribute you are considering. Study them in the sequence listed.

Look up each verse or passage in two or three translations, if possible, and meditate carefully on each one. Meditation, a key ingredient of this study, involves taking time to allow God to speak to you. In your meditation, analyze what each verse is saying by emphasizing different words in the verse, by putting the verse into your own words, and by asking your own questions about it. As truths about God stand out to you, examine your life and see what bearing they may have on your attitudes and actions. As you meditate, mark in your Bible the things that most impress you.

2. FAVORITE PASSAGES

Copy from your Bible the verses or parts of verses that mean the most to you from the *Verses to Consider* part above.

Reexamine the passages you have marked, and choose the verses or phrases that most help you understand and feel the reality of the truth you are studying. Copy these in this part of your study.

Aim to record a few truths that particularly impress you rather than copying every passage. After you tune your heart to this aspect of the person of God, you will be more alert to finding additional Scriptures as you have your quiet time, listen to sermons, and discuss the Word with your friends. By adding new verses when you find them, you can expand your study in the coming days, months, and even years.

Take time to appreciate and worship God in connection with the truths you are discovering about Him. Appreciation and worship are vitally important—they uplift your spirit and bring pleasure and glory to God. Cultivate the habit of turning to the *Favorite Passages* parts of your studies for further reflection and praise. You can do this at the beginning of your quiet time, in family devotions, or before going to bed. Return to these parts also when you need refreshment or your faith needs strengthening.

For the topic "God's Sovereignty," your *Favorite Passages* part might look like this:

2. Favorite Passages: Copy from your Bible the verses or parts of verses that mean the most to you from the previous part *Verses to Consider*. (In the future, add other Scriptures that speak to you in a definite way about God's sovereignty. Use this part often for meditation and praise.)

All the inhabitants of the earth are accounted as nothing,
But He does according to His will in the host of heaven
And among the inhabitants of earth;
And no one can ward off His hand
Or say to Him, "What have you done?" (Daniel 4:35)

World events are under His control. (Daniel 2:21, TLB)

And we know that all things work together for good [everything that
happens fits into a pattern for good — Phillips], to them that love God,
to them who are the called according to his purpose. (Romans 8:28, KJV)

3. Observations, Illustrations, and Quotations

After you copy your favorite passages, meditate on them, asking the Lord for fresh understanding. Think about the meanings phrase by phrase. (Use a dictionary to clarify the definition of words you do not fully understand.) Record your main thoughts and meditations in this part. As you continue studying, you may also collect quotations, poems, and illustrations that will enrich your appreciation of the attribute being studied. Be especially alert to ways in which people have learned and demonstrated this truth in daily living—such as Jesus Christ and other Bible personalities, outstanding Christians of the past and present, spiritual leaders, your Christian friends, and you yourself.

4. How This Truth Can Affect My Life (Application)

Pray that you will experience God in your daily life as these Scriptures portray Him. Ask yourself, *In what specific way can this aspect of God's character help me in one of the following areas?*

- In relating to God better
- In overcoming fears and anxieties
- In finding the fulfillment of my longings
- In developing loving attitudes and actions toward others
- In facing discouragement, misunderstanding, and failure
- In overcoming difficulties

For the topic *God's Ability and Power,* your application might read:

4. How This Truth Can Affect My Life (Application)

> *I need to deepen my trust by realizing the truth of God's ability and power, especially when I get anxious about problems (as for now, Robert's struggles in school and our financial pressures). I'm going to memorize Jeremiah 32:17 to use in prayer. Also, I'll copy it on extra verse cards and tape them on the bathroom mirror and next to my bed to remind me of God's unlimited power to work in my situation.*

Applying the Scriptures to daily living is the most important result of Bible study. Application in this study answers the question, What does this aspect of God's person say to *me*? Many consider this the most valuable part of the study because it provides practical ways to praise and glorify God in everyday life and can become a stepping-stone to greater fruitfulness.

Your application may be drawn from one phrase, one verse, the whole passage, or the whole study. When you write, use the personal, singular pronouns: I, me, my, and mine. Your application should be practical and specific. It should concern a truth you can translate into your daily attitudes, worship, relationships, or activities. State it clearly enough to be understood by anyone who might ask to read it or by the group with whom you might share it.

5. Future Study

During such activities as church services, Bible studies, or informal discussions, you may come across passages of Scripture that apply to the topic under study. You may not have time to copy them in the *Favorite Passages* parts, so jot down the references in this part.

Now you are ready to do the *Experiencing God Study* for the first chapter, "God's Greatness and Majesty" (pages 23-28). The questions in each chapter follow the same format described in the previous instructions, so you will quickly become familiar with the procedure as you continue through this book. Therefore, in order for the study to be challenging and refreshing chapter by chapter, it is important that you think *carefully* and *creatively* about your answers. Don't let your study become routine and uninteresting. Spend time in purposeful meditation, have an open, expectant mind and heart, and see the riches of the Scriptures unfold!

If you complete the *Experiencing God Study* for any chapter and decide to spend more time studying the topic for that chapter, go to the instructions on pages 17-22 for the *Additional Experiencing God Study*.

HOW TO DO
THE *ADDITIONAL*
EXPERIENCING GOD STUDY

T HE OPTIONAL *ADDITIONAL EXPERIENCING God Study* has been designed to help you go deeper as you get to know God better and as you apply what you have learned. It is divided into seven sections and challenges you to study and meditate on the same attribute of God in greater depth and with more participation than in the initial study. You will learn further methods for studying the Bible. You will also understand in a fuller way how the character of God relates to your own life and to the lives of those around you.

1. LOOK UP THE FOLLOWING VERSES. Meditate on them, and then add the most meaningful portions to your *Favorite Passages*. As an option, find additional verses on your own.

Refer again to the instructions for *Verses to Consider* and *Favorite Passages* on page 12. For additional verses, use cross-references from your own memory, the margins of your Bible, or a concordance. If you desire to meditate more intensively, use the six great observation questions: Who? What? When? Where? Why? How? The following sample questions give you ideas on how to do this. Use as few or as many as are helpful.

- WHO?
  According to this passage, *who* can experience this attribute of God?
- WHAT?
  What adjectives describe this attribute?
  What attitudes or actions on God's part spring from it?

- WHEN?

  When do I especially need this attribute?

- WHERE?

  Where in my life can I expect God to demonstrate this attribute?

- WHY?

  Why is it important to understand and experience this attribute?

  Why do I need it?

- HOW?

  How did this truth affect the lives of people in this passage?

  How can I more fully experience this attribute of God?

  How can it influence my view of myself?

Jot down on another piece of paper the insights you want to remember. This will help you study and meditate more effectively.

2. WRITE A PARAGRAPH or simple outline summarizing what your *Favorite Passages* (and possibly other verses you have considered) say about this attribute of God.

In your summary paragraph or outline, briefly state in your own words the important points from the passages. In this part do not include any personal ideas or interpretations, but only what the Bible actually says. An example for the topic "God's Sovereignty" might look like this in summary form:

> *God rules over all beings in heaven and earth (even the greatest of rulers) and works in all that happens (including world events, devastating natural forces, and evil human plans). Absolutely nothing can interfere when He chooses to act. He promises to carry out His purposes, working especially for the good of those who love Him.*

Sometimes you may enjoy making a summary outline, recording first the main divisions of the topic, then briefly summarizing the contents of the verses under these headings. For the topic "God's Sovereignty," your major headings might be:

> *I. The Extent of God's sovereign Control*
>
> *II. The Results of God's Rule*

3. Because many people do not realize how great and majestic God is [or the particular attribute you are studying], what unrealistic ideas do they have about God, about life itself, or about themselves?

Answer this question from your observations of people around you and possibly from books, magazines, and the media. Some sample answers might be:

On *God's Ability and Power:*

Some people think, I am able to handle my own problems and plan my own life. I don't need God.

On *God's Love and Compassion:*

Many people feel that God is unfair and unloving or He wouldn't have let evil things happen to them.

On *God's Holiness and Moral Perfection:*

Some people today believe that God is an impersonal force and therefore amoral. This does away with absolute standards of right and wrong and with a basis for true justice.

4. Answer one or both of the following:

   a. What specific false thoughts and disturbing emotions hinder me when I don't trust [the attribute being studied]? What situations or memories most frequently stimulate these thoughts and feelings?

   b. Although my conscious mind may agree that God is [this attribute], does my outward life demonstrate that He is? What specific attitudes or actions might make people doubt that God is [this attribute] in my estimation?

For a., one answer on the topic of "God's Love and Compassion" might be:

I often think that God could not love such an unworthy person as I. This makes me feel self-condemning and extremely discouraged. I feel this most strongly when I lose my temper, overindulge my appetites, or waste time.

For b., a possible answer on the same topic might be:

My complaining when things go wrong shows that I often do not believe that God is truly loving, that He has my best interests at heart in what He allows to happen to me.

5. WRITE A BRIEF STATEMENT about [this attribute of God] for on-the-spot use in respect to the need you acknowledged in question 4.

This statement can help you get a grip on each truth in a usable way, so that it can rescue you when contrary thoughts or feelings arise within you. Decide first which verse, passage, or thought most powerfully moves you to trust God in regard to your need, then do one of the following:

a. Copy the verse or part of it:

"I am indeed concerned about you" (Exodus 3:16).

b. Rewrite the verse in personalized form, using a personal pronoun:

The Lord is indeed concerned about me (Exodus 3:16, personalized).

c. Make your own concise statement based on the verse or thought:

God will never let anything happen to me that He won't enable me to cope with.

d. Choose a quote from someone else that touches your heart:

"God is too wise to ever make a mistake, too loving to ever do anything unkind" (source unknown).

"Though the night be dark and dreary, darkness cannot hide from Thee; Thou art He who, never weary, watchest where Thy people be" (James Edmeston).

The object is to have *one* concise statement that moves you deeply in a positive way—one that stimulates confidence, thankfulness, peace, joy, or whatever you need. Because it is brief, you can easily memorize it and meditate on it frequently. Use your statement in times of temptation, need, or failure. Acknowledge what is happening in your thoughts, feelings, or actions, and choose against being "pulled under" or led astray. Then consciously think on your brief statement emphatically, thanking God that it is true. Keep meditating on it until the temptation passes or the need is met.

6. DOES SOMEONE NEAR YOU—a friend, brother, sister, spiritual child—have a need or problem that may relate to not realizing [this attribute of God]? How can you help this person become more clear and excited about this attribute and its practical implications?

This question enables you to use the truth you have learned by sharing it with another person. When you recognize the need of sharing one of God's attributes with someone, be sensitive and loving; avoid a critical spirit or any hint of superiority. Often a tactful question or statement will open up a conversation: "Do you feel this might help you in your present disappointment?" or, "I was wondering if this truth might overcome the fears you mentioned the other day."

In order to share God's attributes with others effectively, you must also be honest. Many times you can first share how you need this truth and how you want it to affect your life. Then you and the other person can pray together about both your needs.

7. PRAY FOR ALERTNESS TO areas in your life that relate to [this attribute of God]. Ask for increasing assurance about this truth, and that it will meet specific needs in your life and in the lives of others.

Your trust in God will deepen as you record the ways you and others have experienced His reality, and later review what you have written. These personal illustrations will also help you share Him more effectively with others.

FUTURE EXPERIENCES OF GOD'S SOVEREIGNTY

THE NEED OR SITUATION	HOW GOD USED THIS TRUTH
May 29-30 — Intense anxiety about a forthcoming exam	After I studied ineffectively for an hour, God brought back to mind my "statement of truth" — I can throw the whole weight of my anxieties upon Him, for I am His personal concern. I took time to praise Him for His concern for me, choosing to let Him take the anxieties. Studied and took the exam with a clear mind and peaceful heart.
Early August — Fuming about never having a real vacation	The Lord reminded me from Psalm 4:1 that He is able to work on my behalf. I visualized Him championing my cause, and prayed about a good vacation in His time. Then, that unexpected, expense-paid trip with all the extra blessings it brought, including gifts of money and clothing, was given to me.

Quotation for Meditation from *The Westminster Shorter Catechism*:

Question: What is the chief end of man?
Answer: Man's chief end is to glorify God and to enjoy Him forever.

Sovereign— lord, master

GOD'S GREATNESS
AND MAJESTY

HOW AMAZING IT IS that God, the Supreme Ruler of all, is tenderly involved with each of His children. He is not like us humans with our limited capacity, our inability to give full attention to many people at one time. He is all-knowing, all-seeing, ever-present, able to focus with love on each one of us individually. God shows no favoritism, for *each* of His children is a favorite.

Prayer

> *Dear Father, I worship You as the Most High God, exalted far above all. I praise You for Your mighty dignity and awesome beauty as King of all kings—for Your majesty that rides forth and wins battles. You are the awesome Champion, the all-powerful Warrior who prevails against His enemies. Your greatness extends to all of Your attributes, including Your limitless love.*
>
> *Lord, as I meditate on the Scriptures in this study, may I see more clearly how great and majestic You are, and may I trust You more deeply and more constantly. Amen.*

1. Verses to Consider: 1 Chronicles 29:11-13; 1 Timothy 6:15-16; Jeremiah 32:17; Psalm 145:1-7; Ephesians 1:20-23 (Col 1:29)

[Handwritten annotations:]

1 Ch 29:11 "everything in heaven and earth is yours." (Ps 89:11)
"you are exalted as head over all." (Rev 5:12-13)
:12 "you are the ruler of all things" (2 Ch 20:6)

V 13.
Now, our God, we give you thanks, and praise your glorious name.

1 T: 6:15-16. God, the blessed and only Ruler, the King of king and Lord of lords. (1 Ti 1:11).

Jer 32:17 Ah, Sovereign Lord .... Nothing is too hard for you.
→ Mt 19:26 (Ge 18:14; Job 42:2 Zec 8:6; Lk 1:37; 18:27 Ro 4:21)

2. Favorite Passages: Copy from your Bible the verses or parts of verses that mean the most to you from the previous part, *Verses to Consider.* (In the future, add other Scriptures that speak to you in a definite way about God's greatness and majesty. Use this part often for meditation and praise.)

Jeremiah 32:17

Ah, Sovereign Lord, you have made the heavens and the earth by your great power and outstretched arm. Nothing is too hard for you.'

3. Observations, Illustrations, and Quotations

4. How This Truth Can Affect My Life (Application)

5. Future Study

Extra space for writing answers:

NOTE: If you are able to spend more time on this topic, go on to the following pages. (Instructions are on pages 17-22.)

CHAP. 1 / CONTINUED
GOD'S GREATNESS AND MAJESTY

1. Look up the following verses. Meditate on them, and then add the most meaningful portions to your *Favorite Passages*. As an option, find additional verses on your own.

   Malachi 1:11; Isaiah 40:12-26

2. Write a paragraph or simple outline summarizing what your *Favorite Passages* (and possibly other verses you have considered) say about God's greatness and majesty.

3. Because many people do not realize how great and majestic God is, what unrealistic ideas do they have about God, about life itself, or about themselves?

4. Answer one or both of the following:

a. What specific false thoughts and disturbing emotions hinder me when I don'tfocus on God's greatness and majesty? What situations or memories most frequently stimulate these thoughts and feelings?

b. Although my conscious mind may agree that God is great and majestic, does my outward life demonstrate that He is? What specific attitudes or actions might make people doubt that God is great and majestic in my estimation?

5. Write a brief statement about God's greatness and majesty for on-the-spot use in respect to the need you acknowledged in question 4.

6. Does someone near you—a friend, brother, sister, spiritual child—have a need or problem that may relate to not realizing God's greatness and majesty? How can you help this person become more clear and excited about this attribute and its practical implications?

7. Pray for alertness to areas in your life that relate to God's greatness and majesty. Ask for increasing assurance about this truth, and that it will meet specific needs in your life and in the lives of others.

FUTURE EXPERIENCES OF GOD'S GREATNESS AND MAJESTY

THE NEED OR SITUATION	HOW GOD USED THIS TRUTH

Extra space for writing answers:

GOD'S BEAUTY AND DESIRABILITY

I MAGINE THE MOST BEAUTIFUL vista you have ever seen. Recall the flavor of your favorite food or delicacy. Call to mind a captivating fragrance—a rose, home-baked bread, a pine forest, or some other splendor. All of these things add incredible richness and joy to our lives. Indeed, the most marvelous sights, sounds, smells, and tastes were created by our loving God for our pleasure and His. If we will only pause and be consciously aware of our surroundings, we'll be constantly reminded that our Father overflows with beauty, creativity, and magnificence.

Prayer

Dear Lord, You rise far above all else that I delight in. You are better than a brilliant sunset or starry night, more majestic than towering mountains, more mighty than breakers of the sea. You are more intimate and dear than the sweetest of earthly ties. If I could combine the most wonderful traits of all into one person, this person would in no way compare with You!

Lord, as I feed on Your Word through this study, open my eyes to see how beautiful and desirable You are. Enable me to delight in You more than I ever have before. Amen.

1. Verses to Consider: Psalm 27:4; Song of Solomon 5:16; Psalm 45:2; Philippians 3:7-8; Psalm 36:7-9

2. Favorite Passages: Copy from your Bible the verses or parts of verses that mean the most to you from the previous part *Verses to Consider*. (In the future, add other Scriptures that speak to you in a definite way about God's beauty and desirability. Use this part often for meditation and praise.)

3. Observations, Illustrations, and Quotations

4. How This Truth Can Affect My Life (Application)

5. Future Study

Extra space for writing answers:

_____

NOTE: If you are able to spend more time on this topic, go on to the following pages. (Instructions are on pages 17-22.)

CHAP. 2 / CONTINUED
GOD'S BEAUTY AND DESIRABILITY

1. Look up the following verses. Meditate on them, and then add the most meaningful portions to your *Favorite Passages*. As an option, find additional verses on your own.

   Psalm 63:1-5; 1 Peter 2:4,6-7; Psalm 61:2-4; 73:25-26; Song of Solomon 2:3-4; Psalm 94:18-19

2. Write a paragraph or simple outline summarizing what your *Favorite Passages* (and possibly other verses you have considered) say about God's beauty and desirability.

3. Because many people do not realize how beautiful and desirable God is, what unrealistic ideas do they have about God, about life itself, or about themselves?

4. Answer one or both of the following:

a. What specific false thoughts and disturbing emotions hinder me when I don't focus on God's beauty and desirability? What situations or memories most frequently stimulate these thoughts and feelings?

b. Although my conscious mind may agree that God is beautiful and desirable, does my outward life demonstrate that He is? What specific attitudes or actions might make people doubt that God is beautiful and desirable in my estimation?

5. Write a brief statement about God's beauty and desirability for on-the-spot use in respect to the need you acknowledged in question 4.

6. Does someone near you—a friend, brother, sister, spiritual child—have a need or problem that may relate to not realizing God's beauty and desirability? How can you help this person become more clear and excited about this attribute and its practical implications?

7. Pray for alertness to areas in your life that relate to God's beauty and desirability. Ask for increasing assurance about this truth, and that it will meet specific needs in your life and in the lives of others.

FUTURE EXPERIENCES OF GOD'S BEAUTY AND DESIRABILITY

THE NEED OR SITUATION	HOW GOD USED THIS TRUTH

Extra space for writing answers:

GOD'S
KNOWABILITY

THE LORD SAYS IN Jeremiah, "Let him who boasts boast of this, that he understands and knows Me, that I am the LORD" (9:24). The highest distinction, the greatest advantage, the crown of our lives is the honor of knowing this exalted, supreme Creator—knowing Him personally and intimately. There is none like Him in greatness or might or wisdom. What an astounding privilege it is to enjoy a close relationship with Him!

Prayer

I rejoice, Lord, that the time is coming when my mind will be stayed on You with not a hint of distraction but with endless delight and perfect peace. And how grateful I am that even now I can fix my mind on You. I can trust You and choose to place my hope in You alone, for You are the Lord God, my everlasting Rock.

Thank You, Father, that I can know You in my mind, grasping ever more fully the wonders of Your Person. And I can know You in my heart, in my spirit, where I can experience You far beyond what words can express.

I pray that You will open my eyes as I study Your knowability and that in special ways my understanding of You will grow deeper and richer. Amen.

1. Verses to Consider: Jeremiah 29:13; 9:23-24; 1 Corinthians 2:11-12; 1 John 5:20; 2 Corinthians 4:6

2. Favorite Passages: Copy from your Bible the verses or parts of verses that mean the most to you from the previous part, *Verses to Consider.* (In the future, add other Scriptures that speak to you in a definite way about God's knowability. Use this part often for meditation and praise.)

3. Observations, Illustrations, and Quotations

4. How This Truth Can Affect My Life (Application)

5. Future Study

Extra space for writing answers:

NOTE: If you are able to spend more time on this topic, go on to the following pages. (Instructions are on pages 17-22.)

CHAP. 3 / CONTINUED
GOD'S KNOWABILITY

1. Look up the following verses. Meditate on them, and then add the most meaningful portions to your *Favorite Passages*. As an option, find additional verses on your own.

   Proverbs 2:1-6; Ephesians 1:17-19; Isaiah 43:10; 2 Peter 3:18; Hosea 6:3

2. Write a paragraph or simple outline summarizing what your *Favorite Passages* (and possibly other verses you have considered) say about God's knowability.

3. Because many people do not realize how knowable God is, what unrealistic ideas do they have about God, about life itself, or about themselves?

4. Answer one or both of the following:

    a. What specific false thoughts and disturbing emotions hinder me when I don't focus on God's knowability? What situations or memories most frequently stimulate these thoughts and feelings?

    b. Although my conscious mind may agree that God is knowable, does my outward life demonstrate that He is? What specific attitudes or actions might make people doubt that God is knowable in my estimation?

5. Write a brief statement about God's knowability for on-the-spot use in respect to the need you acknowledged in question 4.

6. Does someone near you—a friend, brother, sister, spiritual child—have a need or problem that may relate to not realizing God's knowability? How can you help this person become more clear and excited about this attribute and its practical implications?

7. Pray for alertness to areas in your life that relate to God's knowability. Ask for increasing assurance about this truth, and that it will meet specific needs in your life and in the lives of others.

FUTURE EXPERIENCES OF GOD'S KNOWABILITY

THE NEED OR SITUATION	HOW GOD USED THIS TRUTH

Extra space for writing answers:

GOD'S ABILITY AND POWER

W E OFTEN HEAR MEDIA commentators and political analysts refer to the president of the United States as the most powerful person in the Western world—perhaps the entire world. The commander in chief can direct vast armies, create economic policies, and bring about laws that affect millions of people. Yet he is often limited by Congress and by possible responses at the polls. When natural disasters occur, what can a human being do? Despite great resources at his fingertips, a president can do nothing to stop earthquakes, hurricanes, or volcanoes.

There is, of course, one Person whose power and authority know no limits. God has unfettered ability to control world events, regulate the ocean tides, and keep planets spinning in their orbits. Nothing is beyond His reach or the scope of His power. And here is perhaps the most amazing thing of all: this unimaginably powerful God loves you intimately and cares for the smallest details of your life. He is awesome indeed!

Prayer

Lord, I worship You as the greatest, most amazing being—more impressive than all the wonders of the earth, more powerful than all its evil. You are exalted high above any mountains, hindrances, or adversaries that loom large in my life right now. And You are the Overcomer, the Almighty Conqueror, able to win overwhelming victories.

I praise You that You have established the entire universe and You keep it running smoothly. Because this is true, I know that You are infinitely more than able to meet all my needs and work out each difficult or puzzling situation in my life. As I complete this study of Your power and ability, I ask You to deepen and expand my faith in You as the all-powerful, all-loving God. Amen.

1. Verses to Consider: Jeremiah 32:27; Psalm 33:6,9; Mark 10:27; Ephesians 1:19-21; 3:20; Amos 4:13

2. Favorite Passages: Copy from your Bible the verses or parts of verses that mean the most to you from the previous part, *Verses to Consider.* (In the future, add other Scriptures that speak to you in a definite way about God's ability and power. Use this part often for meditation and praise.)

3. Observations, Illustrations, and Quotations

4. How This Truth Can Affect My Life (Application)

5. Future Study

Extra space for writing answers:

_____

NOTE: If you are able to spend more time on this topic, go on to the following pages. (Instructions are on pages 17-22.)

CHAP. 4 / CONTINUED
GOD'S ABILITY AND POWER

1. Look up the following verses. Meditate on them, and then add the most meaningful portions to your *Favorite Passages*. As an option, find additional verses on your own.

   Mark 4:35-41; Psalm 135:5-6; Job 42:2; Hebrews 1:3; Jude 24; Romans 4:20-21

2. Write a paragraph or simple outline summarizing what your *Favorite Passages* (and possibly other verses you have considered) say about God's ability and power.

3. Because many people do not realize how able and powerful God is, what unrealistic ideas do they have about God, about life itself, or about themselves?

4. Answer one or both of the following:
   a. What specific false thoughts and disturbing emotions hinder me when I don't focus on God's ability and power? What situations or memories most frequently stimulate these thoughts and feelings?

   b. Although my conscious mind may agree that God is able and powerful, does my outward life demonstrate that He is? What specific attitudes or actions might make people doubt that God is able and powerful in my estimation?

5. Write a brief statement about God's ability and power for on-the-spot use in respect to the need you acknowledged in question 4.

6. Does someone near you—a friend, brother, sister, spiritual child—have a need or problem that may relate to not realizing God's ability and power? How can you help this person become more clear and excited about this attribute and its practical implications?

7. Pray for alertness to areas in your life that relate to God's ability and power. Ask for increasing assurance about this truth, and that it will meet specific needs in your life and in the lives of others.

FUTURE EXPERIENCES OF GOD'S ABILITY AND POWER

The Need or Situation	How God Used This Truth

Extra space for writing answers:

GOD'S LOVE
AND COMPASSION

I S THERE ANY TRUTH greater than the fact that God loves us? And that He let His Son go through the agonies of the Cross so we could experience that love? His love for us is limitless and endless and infinitely better than any earthly love.

Because of what Christ endured on the cross, His lovingkindness surrounds each of His children like a new atmosphere to live in—an atmosphere of pure, unfailing love that is fresh every morning. How delightful it is to count on the greatness of God's love and settle into its warm intimacy. What an incredible blessing that His love endures forever and will follow us all the days of our lives!

Prayer

I worship You, Lord, thanking You for not simply loving mankind as a mass, as a vast group of people. Your love toward each of Your children—including me—is intensely personal. And how wonderful, too, that Your love extends to each individual in the whole world!

Lord, I place my trust in You, my God of unending compassion, faithfulness, and love. I choose to rest in the knowledge that You are able to resolve my problems and meet my every need. As I work through this study, cause me to be more deeply rooted and more solidly grounded in Your love and kindness. Amen.

1. Verses to Consider: 1 John 3:1-2; 4:9-10; Jeremiah 31:3; Deuteronomy 33:12; Romans 8:35-39

2. Favorite Passages: Copy from your Bible the verses or parts of verses that mean the most to you from the previous part, *Verses to Consider*. (In the future, add other Scriptures that speak to you in a definite way about God's love and compassion. Use this part often for meditation and praise.)

3. Observations, Illustrations, and Quotations

4. How This Truth Can Affect My Life (Application)

5. Future Study

Extra space for writing answers:

NOTE: If you are able to spend more time on this topic, go on to the following pages. (Instructions are on pages 17-22.)

CHAP. 5 / CONTINUED
GOD'S LOVE AND COMPASSION

1. Look up the following verses. Meditate on them, and then add the most meaningful portions to your *Favorite Passages*. As an option, find additional verses on your own.

   Zephaniah 3:17; Hosea 2:19-20; John 15:9-15; Isaiah 54:10; Romans 5:5,8

2. Write a paragraph or simple outline summarizing what your *Favorite Passages* (and possibly other verses you have considered) say about God's love and compassion.

3. Because many people do not realize how loving and compassionate God is, what unrealistic ideas do they have about God, about life itself, or about themselves?

4. Answer one or both of the following:
   a. What specific false thoughts and disturbing emotions hinder me when I don't focus on God's love and compassion? What situations or memories most frequently stimulate these thoughts and feelings?

   b. Although my conscious mind may agree that God is loving and compassionate, does my outward life demonstrate that He is? What specific attitudes or actions might make people doubt that God is loving and compassionate in my estimation?

5. Write a brief statement about God's love and compassion for on-the-spot use in respect to the need you acknowledged in question 4.

6. Does someone near you—a friend, brother, sister, spiritual child—have a need or problem that may relate to not realizing God's love and compassion? How can you help this person become more clear and excited about this attribute and its practical implications?

7. Pray for alertness to areas in your life that relate to God's love and compassion. Ask for increasing assurance about this truth, and that it will meet specific needs in your life and in the lives of others.

FUTURE EXPERIENCES OF GOD'S LOVE AND COMPASSION

The Need or Situation	How God Used This Truth

Extra space for writing answers:

GOD'S HOLINESS AND MORAL PERFECTION

D O YOU KNOW SOMEONE—a pastor, missionary, family member—whom you would describe as "holy"? We rightly admire those individuals who take seriously God's commandments and strive to live righteous, virtuous lives. Still, the man or woman with the most refined character and purity of heart reflects only the slightest resemblance to the holiness of God, for He alone is completely blameless and just.

It was A. W. Tozer who said, "We cannot grasp the true meaning of divine holiness by thinking of someone or something very pure and then raising the concept to the highest degree we are capable of. God's holiness is not simply the best we know infinitely bettered. It stands apart, unique, unapproachable, incomprehensible, and unattainable."[1]

Prayer

Dear Father, You are so holy, so pure, so righteous, and so utterly trustworthy; and by Your doing I am in Christ Jesus. You have given me a deep union, an inner oneness with Him, showering me with Your holiness and purity! You've done this by giving me Your Holy Spirit and Your Holy Son—by planting Your nature in this newly created part of me. You have given me the Spirit of sonship, so that more and more I can bear Your image and resemble You.

Now, Lord, I long to be more like You in my daily living, pure and undefiled, clothed with the glorious beauty of holiness. As I meditate on the truths in this study, show me in life-changing ways the wonders of who You are as my Holy God and Father. Amen.

---

1. A. W. Tozer quoted in *The New Encyclopedia of Christian Quotations* (Grand Rapids, Mich.: Baker Books, 2000), p. 420.

1. Verses to Consider: Exodus 15:11; Deuteronomy 32:4; Hebrews 7:26; 4:15; Psalm 99:3,5,9

2. Favorite Passages: Copy from your Bible the verses or parts of verses that mean the most to you from the previous part, *Verses to Consider.* (In the future, add other Scriptures that speak to you in a definite way about God's holiness and moral perfection. Use this part often for meditation and praise.)

3. Observations, Illustrations, and Quotations

4. How This Truth Can Affect My Life (Application)

5. Future Study

Extra space for writing answers:

_____

NOTE: If you are able to spend more time on this topic, go on to the following pages. (Instructions are on pages 17-22.)

GOD'S HOLINESS AND MORAL PERFECTION

1. Look up the following verses. Meditate on them, and then add the most meaningful portions to your *Favorite Passages*. As an option, find additional verses on your own.

   Revelation 15:4; Isaiah 6:1-3; Psalm 24:3-4; Isaiah 57:15; Hebrews 1:8-9

2. Write a paragraph or simple outline summarizing what your *Favorite Passages* (and possibly other verses you have considered) say about God's holiness and moral perfection.

3. Because many people do not realize how holy and morally perfect God is, what unrealistic ideas do they have about God, about life itself, or about themselves?

4. Answer one or both of the following:

a. What specific false thoughts and disturbing emotions hinder me when I don't focus on God's holiness and moral perfection? What situations or memories most frequently stimulate these thoughts and feelings?

b. Although my conscious mind may agree that God is holy and morally perfect, does my outward life demonstrate that He is? What specific attitudes or actions might make people doubt that God is holy and morally perfect in my estimation?

5. Write a brief statement about God's holiness and moral perfection for on-the-spot use in respect to the need you acknowledged in question 4.

6. Does someone near you—a friend, brother, sister, spiritual child—have a need or problem that may relate to not realizing God's holiness and moral perfection? How can you help this person become more clear and excited about this attribute and its practical implications?

7. Pray for alertness to areas in your life that relate to God's holiness and moral perfection. Ask for increasing assurance about this truth, and that it will meet specific needs in your life and in the lives of others.

FUTURE EXPERIENCES OF GOD'S HOLINESS AND MORAL PERFECTION

THE NEED OR SITUATION	HOW GOD USED THIS TRUTH

Extra space for writing answers:

GOD'S TOTAL
FORGIVENESS

ONE OF THE GREATEST challenges Christians face is learning to forgive others and ourselves. We struggle to let go of wrongs done to us, and we struggle to accept our own faults and failures. Indeed, most of us spend a lifetime learning what it really means to offer and receive forgiveness.

Knowing this makes it all the more amazing that forgiveness is woven into the very fabric of God's nature. His first instinct and inclination is to forgive us. Because of Christ's work of redemption on the cross, God stands ready at any moment to totally forgive our sins and wrongdoings. What a difference it would make in every aspect of our lives if we could fully understand this marvelous attribute of our Father!

Prayer

Thank You, Father, that You have not only passed over my sin judicially— declaring me "not guilty" because my penalty has been paid—but you have also made me righteous by infusing Your Spirit into my heart. I'm so grateful that the person I am through my union with Christ is blameless and without blemish and that You will never again impute or reckon sin against me.

How delighted I am that You have forgiven me! Thank You that on the cross Christ sealed my pardon and set me free from sin's slavery. Now, Lord, as I proceed through this study, open my heart to delight more fully in Your total forgiveness. Amen.

1. Verses to Consider: John 1:29; 1 Peter 2:24; 3:18; Hebrews 8:12; Psalm 103:8-12; Acts 10:43; Romans 8:1,33-34

2. Favorite Passages: Copy from your Bible the verses or parts of verses that mean the most to you from the previous part, *Verses to Consider*. (In the future, add other Scriptures that speak to you in a definite way about God's total forgiveness. Use this part often for meditation and praise.)

3. Observations, Illustrations, and Quotations

4. How This Truth Can Affect My Life (Application)

5. Future Study

Extra space for writing answers:

NOTE: If you are able to spend more time on this topic, go on to the following pages. (Instructions are on pages 17-22.)

CHAP. 7 / CONTINUED
GOD'S TOTAL FORGIVENESS

1. Look up the following verses. Meditate on them, and then add the most meaningful portions to your *Favorite Passages*. As an option, find additional verses on your own.

   Isaiah 53:5-6; 1:18; 1 John 1:9; Romans 4:7-8; Micah 7:18; Psalm 130:3-4

2. Write a paragraph or simple outline summarizing what your *Favorite Passages* (and possibly other verses you have considered) say about God's total forgiveness.

3. Because many people do not realize how totally forgiving God is, what unrealistic ideas do they have about God, about life itself, or about themselves?

4. Answer one or both of the following:

   a. What specific false thoughts and disturbing emotions hinder me when I don't focus on God's total forgiveness? What situations or memories most frequently stimulate these thoughts and feelings?

   b. Although my conscious mind may agree that God is totally forgiving, does my outward life demonstrate that He is? What specific attitudes or actions might make people doubt that God is totally forgiving in my estimation?

5. Write a brief statement about God's total forgiveness for on-the-spot use in respect to the need you acknowledged in question 4.

6. Does someone near you—a friend, brother, sister, spiritual child—have a need or problem that may relate to not realizing God's total forgiveness? How can you help this person become more clear and excited about this attribute and its practical implications?

7. Pray for alertness to areas in your life that relate to God's total forgiveness. Ask for increasing assurance about this truth, and that it will meet specific needs in your life and in the lives of others.

FUTURE EXPERIENCES OF GOD'S TOTAL FORGIVENESS

The Need or Situation	How God Used This Truth

Extra space for writing answers:

GOD'S GOODNESS AND GENEROSITY

ONCE WE SEE THE heart of God as revealed in the Bible, we realize it is not selfish to look to Him to meet our needs. He loves to give. God has no reluctance to extend His compassion and generosity. In no way does His giving deplete Him, and our receptivity frees Him to express His gracious nature more fully to us and others. He wants us to receive by faith all that we need—physically, emotionally, and spiritually. This makes our lives "test tubes" that demonstrate what happens when a loving, powerful God is moved by faith to meet human needs, both small and great.

Prayer

Lord, You are the God of hope, the God of good plans and kind intentions, the God who promises and keeps His word. Open my eyes to see in fresh ways how good and generous You are. And let me see Your goodness in the trials that You allow in my life, which in Your time You will use to enrich me and deepen my trust in You.

Day by day, create in my heart a glad rest in who You are. More and more, produce within me an even flow of love toward You. May nothing, large or small, divert me from responding to You with a settled love and trust in Your goodness. And as I do this study, give me fresh insights into how good and generous You are. Amen.

1. Verses to Consider: Psalms 31:19; 145:7-9; 23:6; 84:11; Romans 8:28-29,32; Jeremiah 29:11

2. Favorite Passages: Copy from your Bible the verses or parts of verses that mean the most to you from the previous part, *Verses to Consider.* (In the future, add other Scriptures that speak to you in a definite way about God's goodness and generosity. Use this part often for meditation and praise.)

3. Observations, Illustrations, and Quotations

4. How This Truth Can Affect My Life (Application)

5. Future Study

Extra space for writing answers:

NOTE: If you are able to spend more time on this topic, go on to the following pages. (Instructions are on pages 17-22.)

CHAP. 8 / CONTINUED
GOD'S GOODNESS AND GENEROSITY

1. Look up the following verses. Meditate on them, and then add the most meaningful portions to your *Favorite Passages*. As an option, find additional verses on your own.

   Psalms 34:8-10; 107:8-9; 103:1-5; James 1:17; Psalm 86:5

2. Write a paragraph or simple outline summarizing what your *Favorite Passages* (and possibly other verses you have considered) say about God's goodness and generosity.

3. Because many people do not realize how good and generous God is, what unrealistic ideas do they have about God, about life itself, or about themselves?

4. Answer one or both of the following:
   a. What specific false thoughts and disturbing emotions hinder me when I don't focus on God's goodness and generosity? What situations or memories most frequently stimulate these thoughts and feelings?

   b. Although my conscious mind may agree that God is good and generous, does my outward life demonstrate that He is? What specific attitudes or actions might make people doubt that God is good and generous in my estimation?

5. Write a brief statement about God's goodness and generosity for on-the-spot use in respect to the need you acknowledged in question 4.

6. Does someone near you—a friend, brother, sister, spiritual child—have a need or problem that may relate to not realizing God's goodness and generosity? How can you help this person become more clear and excited about this attribute and its practical implications?

7. Pray for alertness to areas in your life that relate to God's goodness and generosity. Ask for increasing assurance about this truth, and that it will meet specific needs in your life and in the lives of others.

FUTURE EXPERIENCES OF GOD'S GOODNESS AND GENEROSITY

THE NEED OR SITUATION	HOW GOD USED THIS TRUTH

Extra space for writing answers:

GOD'S SOVEREIGNTY

HOW GOOD IT IS to know that God is sovereign. He is a mighty King who serves as our protector and advocate. He is an avenger, a powerful warrior, a gracious giver. James Bordwine once said, "To say that God is sovereign is to say that His power is superior to every other form or expression of power. It is to say that God is completely free of external influences so that He does what He chooses, as He chooses, when He chooses."[1]

God's sovereignty might be a fearful thing if we didn't have the complete assurance that He is loving, gracious, and kindhearted. Indeed, He always wields His power to act on our behalf and for our good.

Prayer

In this fallen world, Lord, many things come my way that do not originate in Your heart. But nothing comes my way that does not pass through Your loving and sovereign permission, for my good. You work in mysterious ways, Your wonders to perform. It's a joy to know that behind my assortment of weaknesses, stresses, and troubles stands a God of loving sovereignty.

As I study this aspect of Your character, please open my heart in fresh ways to see the wonders of resting in Your loving sovereignty. Amen.

1. Verses to Consider: Isaiah 46:9-10; Daniel 2:20-21; 4:34-35; Matthew 28:18; Romans 8:28

---

1. James Bordwine quoted in *The New Encyclopedia of Christian Quotations* (Grand Rapids, Mich.: Baker Books, 2000), p. 430.

2. Favorite Passages: Copy from your Bible the verses or parts of verses that mean the most to you from the previous part, *Verses to Consider.* (In the future, add other Scriptures that speak to you in a definite way about God's sovereignty. Use this part often for meditation and praise.)

3. Observations, Illustrations, and Quotations

4. How This Truth Can Affect My Life (Application)

5. Future Study

Extra space for writing answers:

NOTE: If you are able to spend more time on this topic, go on to the following pages. (Instructions are on pages 17-22.)

CHAP. 9 / CONTINUED
GOD'S SOVEREIGNTY

1. Look up the following verses. Meditate on them, and then add the most meaningful portions to your *Favorite Passages*. As an option, find additional verses on your own.

   Psalm 33:9-11; Acts 17:26; Revelation 3:7-8; Job 23:13-14; Genesis 50:20

2. Write a paragraph or simple outline summarizing what your *Favorite Passages* (and possibly other verses you have considered) say about God's sovereignty.

3. Because many people do not realize how sovereign God is, what unrealistic ideas do they have about God, about life itself, or about themselves?

4. Answer one or both of the following:

a. What specific false thoughts and disturbing emotions hinder me when I don't focus on God's sovereignty? What situations or memories most frequently stimulate these thoughts and feelings?

b. Although my conscious mind may agree that God is sovereign, does my outward life demonstrate that He is? What specific attitudes or actions might make people doubt that God is sovereign in my estimation?

5. Write a brief statement about God's sovereignty for on-the-spot use in respect to the need you acknowledged in question 4.

6. Does someone near you—a friend, brother, sister, spiritual child—have a need or problem that may relate to not realizing God's sovereignty? How can you help this person become more clear and excited about this attribute and its practical implications?

7. Pray for alertness to areas in your life that relate to God's sovereignty. Ask for increasing assurance about this truth, and that it will meet specific needs in your life and in the lives of others.

FUTURE EXPERIENCES OF GOD'S SOVEREIGNTY

The Need or Situation	How God Used This Truth

Extra space for writing answers:

GOD'S GRACE AND SUFFICIENCY

GRACE IS AN ETERNAL and inherent attitude in God's heart. He gives because He is the one source of all things, and creation would cease to exist if He did not give. But He also gives because it is His unchangeable nature to give freely. It's a delight that He will not relinquish.

We never come to God without needing mercy and grace far more than we know. We must have mercy for the countless ways we still fail to measure up, and grace for the countless things we need but don't deserve. As the hymn writer put it, "All that I am or hope to be, O Son of God, I owe to Thee."[1]

God's grace, not our deserving, has made us what we are. All our service is enabled by Him, so all the glory goes to Him. Never can we come near to giving Him the dividends, the returns, that match His investment. God never owes us anything!

Prayer

Thank You, Father, for the river of grace—all-sufficient grace—that flows from You at all times. I'm so grateful that I can boldly kneel at Your throne of grace, opening my arms wide, baring my soul, and letting Your grace flow in. I can drop my defenses, relax my tensions, and be still, knowing that in You is an infinite supply of grace.

How I long to experience Your grace and sufficiency more fully and more constantly! I pray that You will reveal Yourself to me in special ways as I prayerfully study the Scriptures in this lesson. Amen.

---

1. C. Austin Miles, "In Thee Do I Live" (Chicago, Ill.: The Rodeheaver Co., 1938).

1. Verses to Consider: John 1:14-16; 2 Corinthians 12:9; Ephesians 1:2-8; Hebrews 4:16; 2 Thessalonians 2:16-17

2. Favorite Passages: Copy from your Bible the verses or parts of verses that mean the most to you from the previous part, *Verses to Consider*. (In the future, add other Scriptures that speak to you in a definite way about God's grace and sufficiency. Use this part often for meditation and praise.)

3. Observations, Illustrations, and Quotations

4. How This Truth Can Affect My Life (Application)

5. Future Study

Extra space for writing answers:

_____

NOTE: If you are able to spend more time on this topic, go on to the following pages. (Instructions are on pages 17-22.)

CHAP. 10 / CONTINUED
GOD'S GRACE AND SUFFICIENCY

1. Look up the following verses. Meditate on them, and then add the most meaningful portions to your *Favorite Passages*. As an option, find additional verses on your own.

   2 Peter 1:2-3; Ephesians 2:4-9; Romans 5:17; 2 Corinthians 3:5; 1 Peter 5:10

2. Write a paragraph or simple outline summarizing what your *Favorite Passages* (and possibly other verses you have considered) say about God's grace and sufficiency.

3. Because many people do not realize how gracious and sufficient God is, what unrealistic ideas do they have about God, about life itself, or about themselves?

4. Answer one or both of the following:

a. What specific false thoughts and disturbing emotions hinder me when I don't focus on God's grace and sufficiency? What situations or memories most frequently stimulate these thoughts and feelings?

b. Although my conscious mind may agree that God is gracious and sufficient, does my outward life demonstrate that He is? What specific attitudes or actions might make people doubt that God is gracious and sufficient in my estimation?

5. Write a brief statement about God's grace and sufficiency for on-the-spot use in respect to the need you acknowledged in question 4.

6. Does someone near you—a friend, brother, sister, spiritual child—have a need or problem that may relate to not realizing God's grace and sufficiency? How can you help this person become more clear and excited about this attribute and its practical implications?

7. Pray for alertness to areas in your life that relate to God's grace and sufficiency. Ask for increasing assurance about this truth, and that it will meet specific needs in your life and in the lives of others.

FUTURE EXPERIENCES OF GOD'S GRACE AND SUFFICIENCY

THE NEED OR SITUATION	HOW GOD USED THIS TRUTH

Extra space for writing answers:

GOD'S FAITHFULNESS AND DEPENDABILITY

ONE OF THE MOST beloved hymns of all time beautifully captures an aspect of God's character:

Great is Thy faithfulness, O God my Father
There is no shadow of turning with Thee.
Thou changest not, Thy compassions they fail not.
All Thou hast been, Thou forever will be.[1]

Truer words have never been written. Our Lord is the most dependable and reliable of all beings—the living God who delights to exercise lovingkindness, justice, and righteousness. Sometimes in frustration we may complain, "God, where are You? I feel so alone." But, in fact, we are never alone and never abandoned. He walks hand-in-hand with us through every triumph and failure, every victory and defeat. Great is His faithfulness indeed!

Isa 41:10,13

Prayer

I am so grateful, Lord, that I can utterly rely on You, knowing that You will always be faithful. You have linked me with Yourself, so that I know You in loving, mutual commitment. What more could I want to assure me that I am all right—that I am important, secure, cared for? I rejoice that even when I encounter situations that are painful and appear unfair, You never fail to be dependable and trustworthy.

2Ti 2:13

Gracious Father, use this study to deepen my knowledge of You and my confidence in You. Amen.

---

1. Thomas O. Chisholm, William M. Runyan, "Great Is Thy Faithfulness" (Carol Stream, Ill.: Hope Publishing, 1923).

1. Verses to Consider: Lamentations 3:22-23; Numbers 23:19; Hebrews 6:17-19; Deuteronomy 7:9; Psalm 89:1-2

2. Favorite Passages: Copy from your Bible the verses or parts of verses that mean the most to you from the previous part, *Verses to Consider* part above. (In the future, add other Scriptures that speak to you in a definite way about God's faithfulness and dependability. Use this part often for meditation and praise.)

Lam 3:21 Yet this I call to mind and *therefore* I have hope.

:22 Because of the Lord's great love we are not consumed for his compassions *never fail*. (Ps 78:38).

✓:23 They are new *every morning*; great is your *faithfulness*.

✱ Zeph 3:5 (morning by morning / every new day he does not fail)

Divine Faithfulness → Dt 7:9; 1Ki 8:56; Ps 36:5; 89:1; 1Co 1:9; of God. Heb 6:18; 1 Pe 4:19.

of Christ → 1Th 5:24; 2Th 3:3; 2Ti 2:13; Heb 2:17; 10:23; Rev 1:5; ⟨19:11⟩ ⟶ 3:14 → Col 1:15-17

3. Observations, Illustrations, and Quotations

Deut 7:9 Know therefore, that the Lord your God is God; he is the faithful God Keeping his covenant of love to a thousand generations of those who love him and keep his commands.

✱Rev-19:11 - Christ Faithful / Christ the Judge / Spiritual Warfare.

v11. ⟵ 1Timothy 6:12. "Fight the good fight of the faith. Take hold of the eternal to which you were called when you made your good confession in the presence of many witnesses.

4. How This Truth Can Affect My Life (Application)

5. Future Study

Extra space for writing answers:

NOTE: If you are able to spend more time on this topic, go on to the following pages. (Instructions are on pages 17-22.)

CHAP. 11 / CONTINUED
GOD'S FAITHFULNESS AND DEPENDABILITY

1. Look up the following verses. Meditate on them, and then add the most meaningful portions to your *Favorite Passages*. As an option, find additional verses on your own.

   Philippians 1:6; 1 Thessalonians 5:23-24; 2 Thessalonians 3:3; Isaiah 49:14-16; Joshua 21:45; Psalm 119:89-91

2. Write a paragraph or simple outline summarizing what your *Favorite Passages* (and possibly other verses you have considered) say about God's faithfulness and dependability.

3. Because many people do not realize how faithful and dependable God is, what unrealistic ideas do they have about God, about life itself, or about themselves?

4. Answer one or both of the following:

a. What specific false thoughts and disturbing emotions hinder me when I don't focus on God's faithfulness and dependability? What situations or memories most frequently stimulate these thoughts and feelings?

b. Although my conscious mind may agree that God is faithful and dependable, does my outward life demonstrate that He is? What specific attitudes or actions might make people doubt that God is faithful and dependable in my estimation?

5. Write a brief statement about God's faithfulness and dependability for on-the-spot use in respect to the need you acknowledged in question 4.

6. Does someone near you—a friend, brother, sister, spiritual child—have a need or problem that may relate to not realizing God's faithfulness and dependability? How can you help this person become more clear and excited about this attribute and its practical implications?

7. Pray for alertness to areas in your life that relate to God's faithfulness and dependability. Ask for increasing assurance about this truth, and that it will meet specific needs in your life and in the lives of others.

FUTURE EXPERIENCES OF GOD'S FAITHFULNESS AND DEPENDABILITY

The Need or Situation	How God Used This Truth

Extra space for writing answers:

GOD'S WORTHINESS AND GLORY

THE PSALMIST TELLS US that "the heavens are telling of the glory of God" (19:1). Later, we read that the angels sang in a loud voice, "Worthy is the Lamb that was slain to receive . . . honor and glory and blessing!" (Revelation 5:12). These two attributes of God—worthiness and glory—are woven throughout Scripture as the biblical writers use the most beautiful and powerful language possible to convey how magnificent the Lord is.

Though we are privileged to call God our friend, we must also give Him all the respect, reverence, and adoration befitting a King, for that is exactly what He is.

Prayer

Lord, I bow before You in humility, for You are high and lofty and infinitely greater than I am. I am poor and needy, unable even to exist apart from You. Indeed, You hold together every cell and organ of my body. I can do nothing that is pleasing in Your sight except as I abide in Your Son and He in me.

You are almighty and all holy—the most glorious One, who is altogether desirable. And You are the source of all that we need. All good things come from You and You reign over all. So I come before You, contrite and humble, submitting to You. I open myself to receive in my whole being Your presence, Your will, and Your plan for me, with its joys and sufferings.

As I do this study, grant me the grace of seeing in a life-changing way how worthy and glorious You are. Amen.

1. Verses to Consider: Revelation 4:11; 5:12-14; Colossians 1:15-20; Psalm 96:7-10; Jeremiah 10:6-7

2. Favorite Passages: Copy from your Bible the verses or parts of verses that mean the most to you from the previous part, *Verses to Consider.* (In the future, add other Scriptures that speak to you in a definite way about God's worthiness and glory. Use this part often for meditation and praise.)

3. Observations, Illustrations, and Quotations

4. How This Truth Can Affect My Life (Application)

5. Future Study

Extra space for writing answers:

NOTE: If you are able to spend more time on this topic, go on to the following pages. (Instructions are on pages 17-22.)

CHAP. 12 / CONTINUED
GOD'S WORTHINESS AND GLORY

1. Look up the following verses. Meditate on them, and then add the most meaningful portions to your *Favorite Passages*. As an option, find additional verses on your own.

   2 Peter 1:17; Hebrews 1:6-12; Isaiah 9:6-7; Philippians 2:6-11; Psalms 100; 89:6-8

2. Write a paragraph or simple outline summarizing what your *Favorite Passages* (and possibly other verses you have considered) say about God's worthiness and glory.

3. Because many people do not realize how worthy and glorious God is, what unrealistic ideas do they have about God, about life itself, or about themselves?

4. Answer one or both of the following:

a. What specific false thoughts and disturbing emotions hinder me when I don't focus on God's worthiness and glory? What situations or memories most frequently stimulate these thoughts and feelings?

b. Although my conscious mind may agree that God is worthy and glorious, does my outward life demonstrate that He is? What specific attitudes or actions might make people doubt that God is worthy and glorious in my estimation?

5. Write a brief statement about God's worthiness and glory for on-the-spot use in respect to the need you acknowledged in question 4.

6. Does someone near you—a friend, brother, sister, spiritual child—have a need or problem that may relate to not realizing God's worthiness and glory? How can you help this person become more clear and excited about this attribute and its practical implications?

7. Pray for alertness to areas in your life that relate to God's worthiness and glory. Ask for increasing assurance about this truth, and that it will meet specific needs in your life and in the lives of others.

FUTURE EXPERIENCES OF GOD'S WORTHINESS AND GLORY

THE NEED OR SITUATION	HOW GOD USED THIS TRUTH

Extra space for writing answers:

REVIEWING GOD'S ATTRIBUTES

THIS STUDY GIVES YOU the opportunity to review the attributes you have considered and to focus on the amazing blend of qualities in God.

Prayer

Dear Father, what a privilege it is to know You and understand Your attributes better! As I review these studies, may Your Word grip my heart and change my life in new ways. And as the months and years go by, please continue to enrich my life through the truths I have studied. Amen.

1. Record which attributes you would place in the following categories (not all attributes will be included).

   a. The strong and awesome side of God's person:

   b. The warm and tender side of God's person:

2. Which two or three verses from your *Favorite Passages* most make you appreciate the strong and awesome side of God? Copy the verses and references below:

3. Which two or three verses most inspire your confidence in the warm and tender aspect of God's person? Copy the verses and references below:

4. Which application from your twelve studies do you most want to pray about and use in the coming weeks?

5. Copy or summarize one passage that especially makes you feel that our God is worthy of your total response.

6. What particular area of your life do you want to dedicate to God in view of His worthiness? Anything in respect to your priorities? Your relationships? Your longings? Your future plans? Or your entire self—have you made Him Lord of all?

NOTE: If you are able to spend more time on this topic, go on to the following pages. (Instructions are on pages 17-22.)

REVIEWING GOD'S ATTRIBUTES

1. Review your twelve summaries (question 2 of your Additional Experiencing God Study), and write a short paragraph or outline summarizing what you have learned about God.

2. Review questions 4 and 5 of your additional studies and copy the one "brief statement" that you most want to remember and use.

3. As you think back over the attributes you have studied, write a statement or brief paragraph on *one* of the following questions:

   a. How have these studies helped me overcome misconceptions of God, fears about Him, or feelings against Him?

   b. In what way have these studies affected my thoughts and feelings about myself?

c. What further truths or observations impressed me as I went back over the twelve studies?

4. Consider writing a letter to a friend or young Christian, sharing something that stood out to you in this review. Also ask him to pray for you as you apply that truth (or another) to a particular need in your own life. Write down some names of people to whom you might write:

5. (Optional) In Psalm 145, David pours out his adoration at the delightful combination of awesome majesty and warm compassion that he had discovered in God. Prayerfully read this psalm, seeking to see God as David saw Him and responding as he did. Then record below the words or phrases that describe these two aspects of God.

GOD IS GREAT, MIGHTY, AWESOME	GOD IS TENDER AND COMPASSIONATE

6. (Optional) According to Psalm 145, in view of what God is like:

a. What should you do in direct response to Him?

b. What should you do in relation to people?

With eyes wide open to the mercies of God, I beg you, my brothers, as an act of intelligent worship, to give him your bodies, as a living sacrifice, consecrated to him and acceptable by him. Don't let the world around you squeeze you into its own mould, but let God re-mould your minds from within, so that you may prove in practice that the plan of God for you is good, meets all his demands and moves towards the goal of true maturity.

—ROMANS 12:1-2, PH

I heard His call, "Come, follow."
That was all.
My gold grew dim
My soul went after Him
I rose and followed,
That was all.
Who would not follow
If they heard *Him* call?

—WILLIAM R. NEWELL

FOR FURTHER READING

THE FOLLOWING ARE SOME excellent books on the person of God and having a dynamic relationship with Him:

Myers, Ruth (with Warren Myers). *31 Days of Praise: Enjoying God Anew* (Sisters, Ore.: Multnomah).

Myers, Ruth. *The Perfect Love* (Colorado Springs, Colo.: WaterBrook Press).

Packer, James I. *Knowing God* (Downers Grove, Ill.: InterVarsity).

Peace, Richard. *Learning to Love God* (Colorado Springs, Colo.: NavPress).

Stafford, Tim. *Knowing the Face of God* (Colorado Springs, Colo.: NavPress).

Stone, Nathan J. *The Names of God* (Chicago: Moody).

Tozer, A. W. *The Knowledge of the Holy* (New York: Harper & Row).

Tozer, A. W. *The Pursuit of God* (Harrisburg, Penn.: Christian Publications).

The following are materials on meditation and Bible study from The Navigators, available from your local Christian bookstore.

Downing, Jim. *Meditation: The Bible Tells You How.*

Foster, Robert D. *Seven Minutes with God: How to Plan a Daily Quiet Time* (pamphlet).

Smith, Michael M. *Growing in Faith.*

The Navigator Bible Studies Handbook.

FUTURE STUDY SUGGESTIONS

THIS STUDY HAS ENABLED you to discover some truths about God and His relationship to you. As time goes by, you will think of other characteristics of our Lord—truths about His nature and attributes, His names, titles, and offices, and His concern for you. Whenever you are impressed with a Scripture that brings to mind a quality of His person that you have not yet studied, record your discovery and observations below. This will give you glimpses of God that you may want to study more thoroughly later.

REFERENCES	TRUTHS ABOUT GOD

This study, *Experiencing God's Attributes,* is one of a series of Navigator studies by Warren and Ruth Myers on the person of God and the relationship we can have with Him. The *Experiencing God Series* is published by NavPress.

AUTHORS

WARREN AND RUTH MYERS served on the staff of The Navigators in Asia from 1970 until Warren's promotion to Glory in 2001. Prior to their marriage in 1968, each of them had served as Navigator staff members in Asia and the United States. Ruth continues to serve with The Navigators, living in Colorado Springs.

Warren received Jesus Christ as his personal Savior shortly before the end of World War II while serving in the U.S. Army Air Corps. Following the war, he attended the University of California at Berkeley. In Berkeley, he attended First Presbyterian Church, was involved in Navigator Bible study classes there, and committed himself to being available to serve on the foreign mission field.

After studying religion and mechanical engineering, he graduated in 1949. That same year he attended his first Navigator conference, and was strongly impressed by the emphasis on man-to-man training and spiritual multiplication. Although previously intending to enroll in a seminary, he joined the Navigator staff in Los Angeles for three years of training and ministry.

He went to Asia for The Navigators in 1952, serving in Hong Kong, India, and Vietnam before returning to a staff position in the United States in 1960.

Ruth was led by her mother to receive Christ as Savior at age ten. Following some years of spiritual doubt and questioning, she committed herself at age sixteen to do whatever God might want her to do in life—including missionary work.

After high school she attended Northwestern Bible and Missionary Training School in Minneapolis, Minnesota, where she experienced new joy and vitality in her relationship with Christ. She also met Dean Denler there, who later became her husband and a Navigator staff member.

Following graduation from Bible school, she attended Macalester College in Saint Paul, where she helped in the student ministry of The Navigators. She was involved in Navigator ministries in Washington, D.C., and Minneapolis before going to Taiwan in 1952 to marry Denler. She served with him in Taiwan, the Philippines, and Hong Kong before his death in 1960. She then served at The Navigators headquarters in Colorado Springs, Colorado, until her marriage with Warren.

She and Warren, both gifted Bible teachers, wrote this study from a series of Bible studies on God's attributes that had been used successfully for years, primarily in Ruth's ministry.

MORE ENCOURAGING STUDIES BY WARREN AND RUTH MYERS.

Discovering God's Will

Perfect for anyone seeking to find lasting meaning and purpose, this timely, proven workbook will help you find out what God wants you to do and how to trust Him in the process.

1-57683-178-7

Experiencing God's Presence

Are we supposed to be needy? When it comes to depending upon God to take care of us, the answer is "yes." This study shows how God created us to need and experience His presence in our lives.

1-57683-418-2

To get your copies, visit your local bookstore, call 1-800-366-7788, or log on to www.navpress.com. Ask for a FREE catalog of NavPress products. Offer #BPA.

NAVPRESS
BRINGING TRUTH TO LIFE
w w w . n a v p r e s s . c o m